Go Figure

a DAYS OF SPANIARD story
from

The Spaniard

With lessons and cliffhangers
all along the way

PARENTS | GUARDIANS | TEACHERS
Please consider reading & discussing this book with your child, student or group over 30 days. Turn the page to see the reason.

ISBN 9798376437636

This is a work of fiction based on the life and work of Charlie "THE SPANIARD" Brenneman and blends fact with fiction. Names, characters, places and incidents are products of imagination or are used fictitiously. The Creative Lead for the DAYS OF SPANIARD series is Keith "DREAD" Eldred, who drafts the stories and refines them with THE SPANIARD.

KIDS ARE WORTH TAKING TIME

This book is designed for
parents, guardians and teachers
to share with young people
in short sessions across 30 days.

Of course, instead you can
read the book straight through.

But please consider going slow
and giving your young audience
something special to look back on—
a time when a caring adult
wanted to talk with them
over and over and over.

In the end, DAYS OF SPANIARD
is not about THE SPANIARD.
It's about the days.

See the end of this book for a
TEACHING GUIDE
WITH QUESTIONS
to help meet instructional standards,
teach students life skills,
and measure understanding

Hey, let's dive into a story meant to be told over 30 days!
In the pages of this book, the story is on the RIGHT and lessons that go along are on the LEFT. Enjoy and learn!
Thanks!
- Spaniard

Dedicated to all of the principals
and other school administrators
who give me the huge honor
of meeting their students

Use caution with unknown contacts who appear on your phone or in social media.

1

A text came in from an unknown number asking if it was okay to call me. I took some time to figure out what to do.

I did reply, but I had a good reason.

Texting can be unpredictable and tricky. Ask adults about what they do when texting, especially about their precautions.

2

The text had come into a Google number that I use in business to shield my actual phone number, so I was bold but cautious. I replied, asking if we could do a call at a certain time … but I heard nothing back for several days leading up to that time. I wondered what was going on.

Then I realized why the person hadn't gotten back to me.

Everyone makes mistakes, even adults who try very hard to be role models.

Apologies are important, but try not to be too hard on yourself.

3

There was no reply because I had never sent my text! I must have gotten busy and only *thought* that I had sent it. I quickly rewrote it, apologizing for the delay, and sent it again (for the first time).

The reply came right away!

Always keep in mind how other people see things. While you're being careful, other people are being careful, too. And in much the same way, while you want friends, other people want friends, too.

The person accepted my requested call time, so the call happened soon. The caller introduced himself as Max and said that he had been cautious with his text, not saying anything about himself. Also because it is unusual for someone to give out his number like I had, and because what he had to explain would sound very odd.

What Max had to say did sound odd indeed. I was flabbergasted!

All ages can get excited about toys, though many people enjoy them as "collectibles" rather than for play. They like having them and sometimes displaying them or buying and selling them.

New technologies can be very exciting. And get this: I happen to know someone who knows someone who helped invent 3D-printing! You'll hear more later about my friend Zerby.

5

Max, the person I had just met on the phone, was an entrepreneur who wanted to *make an action figure of me!* He used a new process that required a full body scan that would connect to a 3D printer. Would I be interested in this?

What Max said sounded great! But I quickly found reasons to be cautious.

A business can do exciting and fun things, but the business can only keep going if it brings in more money than it spends.

It's hard to create products, but it can be even harder to sell them, so you have to choose business projects carefully.

I asked Max what his plan would cost me. I didn't know how he was thinking about creating the action figure, and as much as I liked the idea, I had to understand the cost and benefit.

Max's answer was very surprising to me!

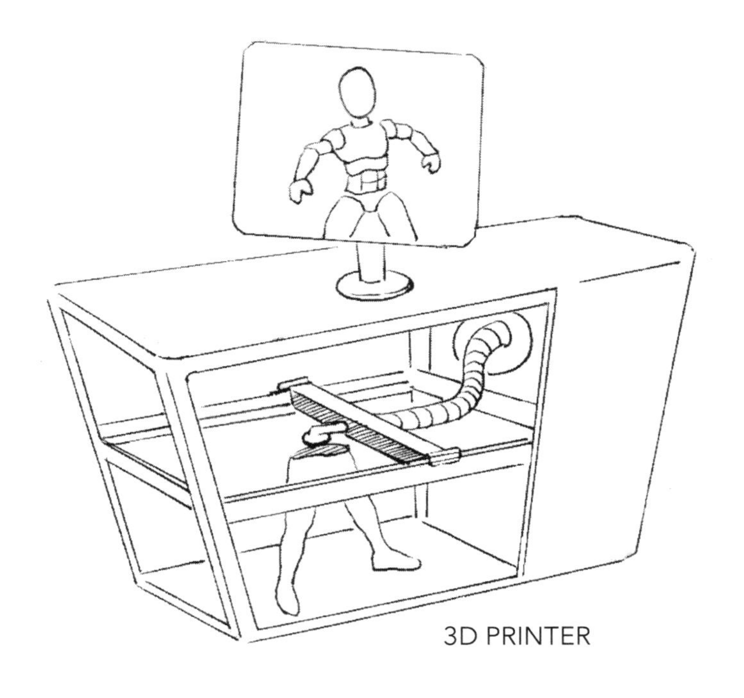

3D PRINTER

Sometimes things do happen that are wonderful and even miraculous. One great example on YouTube is "Caine's Arcade." Search it and watch it!

7

Max said that there would be no cost to me in his plan to turn me into an action figure. He said that he wanted to produce a video about the whole process to use in advertising his 3D printing business. He had looked around online for someone to feature in the video, and he came upon my podcast and videos and liked what I was doing.

Max said that there was another reason that he picked me.

It's rewarding to push yourself to stay strong and healthy, regardless of how far you go in sports.

Max said he wanted to create an action figure of me because he liked my muscles! What he meant is that he liked the fact that I had been a wrestler and fighter and still worked hard to stay in shape. He said that my action figure would look like other action figures of well-known athletes and heroes.

Then Max said that there was still *another* reason that he picked me to become an action figure.

Customs change, and generations sometimes clash. How you treat others of a different age—whether older or younger—matters very much, including if they disagree with you about things like music or tattoos.

Having said that, my advice about tattoos for anyone who wants one is: Think about it for a long time first. Make sure that it is as timeless as possible so it will always have meaning. And ALWAYS go to a trustworthy tattoo artist. A tattoo is there FOR LIFE. Yes, you can get it lasered off, but that can get complicated.

Max said that another reason he wanted to create a Spaniard action figure is because I have tattoos! He was from an earlier generation when tattoos were less common and judged harshly, but he knew that times had changed, and he wanted his action figures to keep up.

And while Max repeated that he liked my tattoos, he also saw a need to approach them on the action figure in a special way. I could hardly believe what he said!

Technology is amazing.

To prepare for a life in technology, here is expert advice from my friend Zerby, who I told you about, whose coworker helped invent 3D printing:

"Building a career in technology is not about building new things for the sake of building new things. It's about *solving problems with powerful tools.* Rather than build technology and then search for problems to solve, search for problems to solve and then build technology. The speed of innovation requires you to constantly be learning new things, and if you don't have a passion for learning, others will pass you by. And remember, at the end of the day, it's people using the technology. *Fall in love with the people you serve.* Make their lives easier with technology, and you'll succeed."

10

Max said he had a way of offering custom tattoos on the action figure. Because it would be small, and because of the way it would be made, it would be hard to have tattoos on the surface at all, much less clear and legible. But his machine could embed tiny sensors to interact with smart phones. At a glance, the figure would have clear skin and no tattoos. But when you looked at the figure through a smartphone camera, tattoos would appear on the skin, and there could be different sets: The actual Spaniard tattoos that I have, custom sets made by others (like tattoo playlists), and individually-customized sets saying whatever a person wanted to see. *(See a picture of this on page 70, but don't read the end of the story yet!)*

I was more pumped than ever! But something was nagging at me. There was a question that I had to ask Max.

It's always better to face concerns head on and as early as possible. If you put off addressing a problem, it can grow and become harder to handle.

11

“Max, what is your full name?” I asked.

“Maximiliano!” he said proudly.

“Where are you from?” I asked.

“I emigrated from the city of Ronda, Spain, as a teen. Now I’m a citizen of both the U.S. and Spain.”

“Wonderful!” I said. “I thought something like that, from your accent. I just want to make sure that you know that I’m not from Spain, and my heritage is not from Spain.”

“What?!” said Max. “But you are *The Spaniard*!”

My heart sank. Would this whole great opportunity disappear?

"Hispanic" has different meanings, but broadly speaking it means the people and culture of Spain or other Spanish-speaking countries.

A fight name is a nickname given to a professional fighter. "The Rock" and "The Spaniard" are fight names—or you could call them ring names.

12

But then Max started laughing. "I'm just kidding you!" he said. "I know you are THE SPANIARD but not *a* Spaniard. I listen to your podcast, I have read your books, I know your story. I don't mind that you are not Hispanic like me. We are both the same: We are proud of where we are from. Your fight name just makes this project that much more special to me."

"Whew! I'm glad you feel that way," I said.

"I'm all ready to say yes," I added. "But here's why I can't."

Take your time with big decisions and get help. Ask people you trust. Others can see things that you can't. Many brains are better than one.

13

"Here's why I can't say yes ... at least not yet," I told Max. "I have to talk to my advisers first, to see what they think. I'll get back to you in two days."

"No problem at all," said Max. "I'll talk to you then."

I immediately started contacting my advisers. *And that includes you!* Think of what you would tell me about the action figure plan, and share that with one of your parents or teachers or another adult. Then read on about what I heard from my advisers and compare all the ideas. The future comes from the ideas that we discuss and follow!

But first I have to tell you something important about gathering advice.

When you make a decision, you might look back on it as good or bad or both. There is no way to make sure ahead of time that a decision is good, so think about it, look at what different choices might cause, get good advice and information, listen to your heart, make a decision and take action. Over time, you will learn more and more about how to make decisions that you can live with and be happy about. Just don't get stuck. Make a decision, and don't look back with regret. Only look back to see what your decision taught you.

Here is a story that I think of when I gather advice. This story is set a long time ago and is said to have come from China.

Once upon a time there was a farmer whose horse ran away. That evening, many of his neighbors dropped by to show their sympathy. "We are so sorry to hear that your horse has run away," they said. "This is most unfortunate."

The farmer said, "Maybe."

The next day the horse came back bringing seven wild horses with it, and in the evening everybody came back and said, "Oh, isn't that lucky! What a great turn of events! Now you have eight horses!"

The farmer again said, "Maybe."

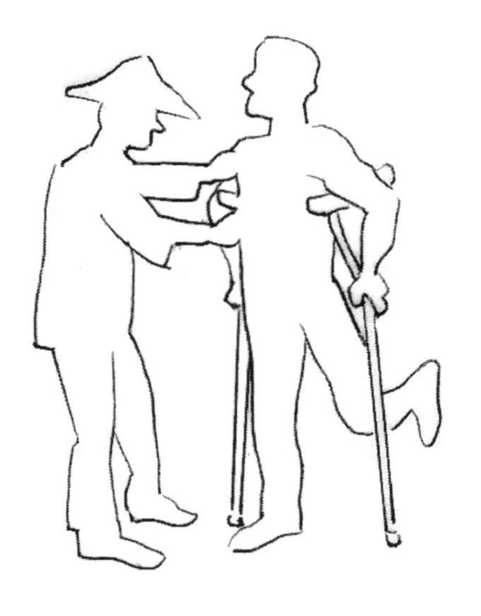

The following day his son tried to break one of the horses for riding, but he was thrown off, fracturing his leg. Then the neighbors said, "Oh dear, that's too bad."

The farmer once again said, "Maybe."

The next day army officers came around to take people into the army, and they rejected the farmer's son because of his broken leg. Again the neighbors came around and said, "Isn't that great!"

You guessed it. The farmer said, "Maybe."

The first person whose opinion I asked for advice about Max's offer was my wife, Amanda.

Those who know us best can help keep us humble and grounded.

At the same time, it means a lot when someone not easily impressed is impressed and sees even a small possibility of good things.

15

My wife Amanda laughed but was happy for me. "Make sure they get your hair right!"

But she added, "In all seriousness, don't get your heart set on this. It's probably like so many other things that people have come to you about over the years. You know as well as I do that they almost never work out like it sounds at first."

It was a good reminder.

Then I asked Dread, my mentor, counselor and mysterious co-creator.

I hope you find, like I have with Dread and a few others, that some people believe in you no matter what.

Paid advertising, like commercials and billboards, is one way that people learn about businesses. News stories are another, and sometimes they can be like free advertising.

16

Dread said, "I'm jealous! That's the greatest thing I ever heard. Think about how your action figure can be different from any other action figure ever, so there will be some news stories about it that help spread the word about you."

Then I asked my old pal Zerby, who understands me from way back and is incredibly creative.

I know it might sound sappy, but so many things trace back to LOVE. Feeling it or not feeling it, receiving it or not receiving it, following it or not following it. Even technology and toys.

Look around you and think about how the things and people that matter in your life show love or a lack of love. Whenever possible, choose LOVE.

17

Zerby is the person I told you about, whose coworker helped invent 3D printing. If you look back at the Lessons in Chapter 10, you'll see his secret to a technology career: It's about creating tools for people you love, to solve their problems.

So in that same email, specifically about Max's creating an action figure of me with changeable tattoos, he said, *"Always be guided by love for students and wanting to help them. Work with Max to do that. That will give the figure its perfect form."*

"POWERFUL," I emailed back.

Then I asked my financial advisor Andy.

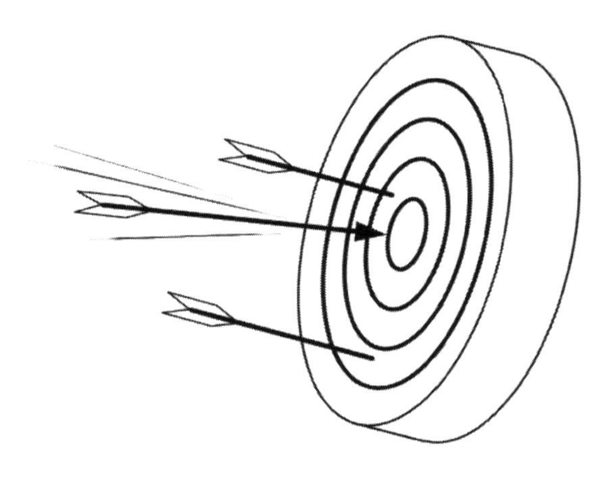

No matter how hard you work, no matter how carefully you aim for a particular goal, you might not hit it, especially when you are trying something new and still learning. But that is never a reason to give up.

Missing a goal can make you hesitate to try again or get stuck preparing. Don't do that! Get ready and just go again. Learn and go, learn and go, again and again. JUST KEEP GOING.

In two words, this idea is FAIL FASTER. That will help you learn faster and succeed faster. It's one of the great secrets of life.

Andy said, "Cool! Understand the deal, but go for it. Like I always say: Ready, Fire, Aim."

I had to laugh. Of course Andy would say that, again. When I first heard it from him, I thought I heard wrong, because the saying is always, "Ready, Aim, Fire." But he meant what he said, in that order. He was telling me not to get stuck, to keep moving.

It was another good reminder.

Then I asked my kids what they thought about their dad becoming an action figure!

Different generations are interested in different things.

Any person of any age can be an important team member. Even a baby! On my podcast "The Spaniard Show," episode 301, I interviewed General John Gronski, whose infant son Stephen crossed the country in a bicycle trailer behind his parents and contributed to the epic family adventure by attracting help from strangers.

Kids! You just never know what they'll say.

The first thing my daughter Gracie said was, "Can Mom be an action figure too?"

My son Rocky said, "So will you have your own movie and video game too?"

I had to tell them no about Mom ("Or at least not right away," I said) and no about the video game and movie ("At least not right away," I repeated).

"Awwww!" they both said, disappointed.

Kids!

Finally, I asked myself what I thought.

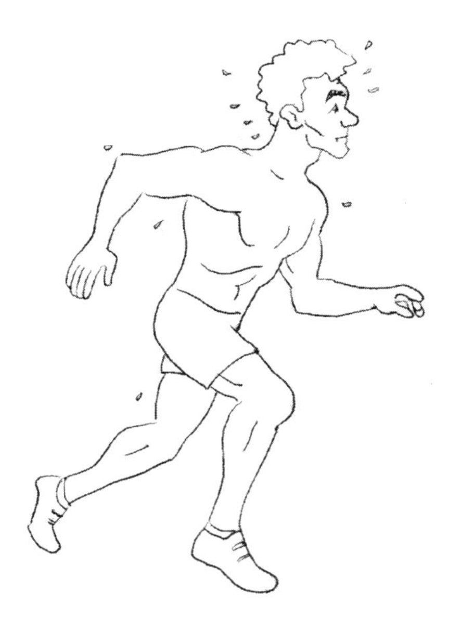

Gathering advice is like gathering stones to build a stone wall. You use a few stones here, a few stones there, and you might decide to leave out some stones entirely because they just don't fit in the wall that you see in your mind. Or you might break some stones into pieces and use some of the pieces but not others. In the end, it's your wall.

20

I went on a long run and thought about everything and put it together in my own way.

Finally I was ready to get back to Max. I knew just what I wanted to tell him and ask him.

How do your ideas compare to what I asked? Soon, you'll see more requests that I made to Max—compare them to your ideas, too.

21

“I want to do it,” I said to Max. “When I go to schools to speak or meet kids at other events, I’d like them to be able to buy a figure of me if they want one. I’d like to have a supply that some kids could win in a drawing. I’d like to keep in touch with you so I can reorder. Also because I hope your technology will get better and better, so that when anyone can have an action figure of themselves produced individually if they like, I can point to your company.”

“There is one more thing,” I said to Max. “Now I’m the one who might sound odd … ”

Asking is an important practice. It can be very hard to do, but it can lead to wonderful things. And the truth is that many people like to receive requests, because they like to help others and share what they have.

22

"I'm fine with everything you said," Max said. "What else did you have in mind?"

I hesitated, because Max had already been generous with his offer, even after I added my requests. I didn't want to push things too far and make him uncomfortable or offend him or even make him regret asking me and turn to someone else. But I had one more request that I felt was the most important of all.

Finally I took a deep breath and asked Max my final question.

When you are trying to come up with ideas, stretch your brain by thinking about opposites. Here are examples: What if chocolate candy wouldn't melt? That gave us M & M's. What if adhesive didn't stick? That gave us Post-It Notes. What if baby toys entertained adults? That is one secret of LEGO. Think opposite! Who knows what you might invent!

23

"Is there such a thing as an INaction figure?" I asked.

"INaction?" said Max.

"Yes," I said. "I wonder if it would be possible to have a second figure that is not in the usual heroic pose. One where I am collapsed on the ground. An action figure and the opposite: An INaction figure."

"A figure of you collapsed?" said Max. "Why in the world would you want that?"

"I have three reasons," I said. "Each of them is an important part of my story that helps kids understand certain things that I want them to know."

Everyone should understand that things can instantly change, for no apparent reason. It's serious to think about, but it can also make you more grateful for every good moment that you have. And it can give you more sympathy for someone whose luck changes.

24

"The first reason that I'd like to also be an INaction figure is that I suffered a stroke during my fighting career. Blood suddenly stopped flowing in part of my brain. I write about this in my first book. Fighting didn't cause the stroke, as far as my doctors could tell, but it happened after I had started training and having professional fights. One minute I was super-healthy, and the next minute I was on the floor helpless."

"Ah, yes, said Max, "I did read about that. What is your second reason?"

Every fighter, and everyone who tries anything difficult, gets knocked down literally or in some way. In the movie "Rocky Balboa," my hero Rocky says to his son something that I say to my son Rocky and my daughter Gracie: "It's about how hard you can get hit and keep moving forward. That's how winning is done!"

Sometimes you can't even keep moving forward. You're down and out. You have to get back up and take the next step.

25

"The second reason I'd like to also be an INaction figure," I said, "is that I was knocked down hard a few times during my fighting career. I wrote about these in my books, too. I suffered a terrible eye injury in practice. I was knocked out on live television and had to recover from a bad concussion."

"Powerful," said Max. "How about the third reason?"

This applies to everyone: Each of us is an action figure AND an inaction figure. A champ and a chump. A winner and a loser. No one has it all together all the time.

26

"The third reason I'd like to also be an INaction figure," I said, "is that I still hit the floor sometimes even though I no longer fight professionally. Sometimes it's circumstances, like a stroke, that drop you. Sometimes it's a competitor or just someone in the right place at the wrong time. And sometimes it's you: Poor habits. Or poor judgment, even if you thought long and hard. But you don't know what you don't know. When it comes down to it, I want anyone who looks at my action figure to see me just as much as an INaction figure: Someone who takes action, but who sometimes get stopped. But someone who never stays down. You just find a way to keep moving."

"This is beautiful!" Max said. "There's only one problem."

There's a saying: Necessity is the mother of invention. That means that when you really need something to exist and it doesn't, you have extra motivation to figure it out. And some would say that needing something and wanting something gives you an extra kind of power to create it.

So don't be discouraged when something you want is impossible. That impossibility can help you find a way to make it possible.

27

My heart sank.

But Max continued, "Well, not a problem. There's only one thing: We have never done this kind of body scan before. Our machine is made for a person standing straight. Or the truth is that since many bodies are similar, we can just use a standard 'hero body.' But we do want to make action figures from any kind of body, in any position, and this will help us figure out how. So we'll do it!"

"Then I think we have a deal!" I said. "Let's work out the details."

"*¡Excelente!*" said Max.

Get ready to see the final results!

28

Now I would love to show you both Spaniard toys ... er, collectibles! ... er, figures! Action and Inaction!

But alas, I can't.

Wait, that's not quite true!

29

I can't show you the Spaniard figures YET. This story will help create them. It will help make the idea come true.

But it's not magic. It's something real, with real power.

Spaniard

30

It's called VISION. Describing something in a way that you can picture it.

I hope this story did that for you—that it helped you see both Spaniard figures in your mind. I can! I literally see how I want to appear in the future: As a hero with my arms up, but also knocked down on the ground. Because I'm going to keep fighting forever, and that's what happens when you fight. The future I want is one where I keep going back and forth between those states.

With as much clarity as you can, picture yourself in the future when things are going well but also when things are not going well. I promise you that doing this will help you become who you want to be.

But I also really do mean that this story will help me have actual action figures of myself, as well as INaction figures! Because stories have that much power.

Stories helped create smartphones. When I was a kid, there were reruns of an old TV show called *Star Trek*. You know Star Trek, with Star Fleet officers on starships. They carried little devices called communicators that they used to speak to anyone anywhere. Back then, they didn't exist, but they were so cool that everyone wanted them.

There was another show called *The Jetsons*. Maybe you've seen it, a cartoon where people have flying cars and video phones. We still don't have flying cars, but we do have video phones now.

Made-up stories like those helped create actual reality, because they helped people picture what they wanted. Many kids who watched those kinds of shows became scientists, engineers, designers and inventors who created smartphones and keep improving them. They worked on what was in the stories until they made the stories come true.

SEIZE
THE DAY

Oh, and guess what? This story that I made up for you also includes at least one thing that is not possible yet, as far as I know: A sensor on an action (or INaction) figure that can make a smartphone see custom tattoos on the figure's skin. But that could be cool! And maybe YOU are the person who will hear this story at a young age and go on to invent that technology.

That's what this story is about: Knowing what you want and creating what you want.

You will do it!

You won't stop until you're in the future that you dream.

You'll get up when you're knocked flat.

You'll rise when you fall.

You'll be an action figure and an INaction figure, but you'll never stay down.

go. Go. GO ! ! !

Invitations from
THE SPANIARD

Please watch for the next DAYS OF SPANIARD book on Amazon. Teachers and other adults can sign up for updates and free, early access at **charliespaniard.com/days**

I'd love to hear what you think of the book! Just leave a review on Amazon or reach out on social media @charliespaniard

Thanks!

- Spaniard

Also, find me on a podcast app! Listen any time to my student podcast **SPANIARD SCHOOL** and grown-ups, please find my talks on books, business and life, plus hundreds of interviews with fascinating guests on **THE SPANIARD SHOW**

About
THE SPANIARD

Charlie "The Spaniard" Brenneman is a dork with muscles and awesome tattoos. He loves his family, reading, training, and Cinnamon Toast Crunch. A former Division I wrestler, Spanish teacher and UFC fighter, The Spaniard lives in his native Pennsylvania with his wife Amanda and their children Gracie and Rocky. His mission to embody and inspire lifelong learning has led him to podcasting, writing and speaking.

SPECIAL BONUS! TEACHING GUIDE

Educational Standards & Discussion Questions

I'm a former teacher. My wife and sister are teachers, and one of my brothers is a principal. I create DAYS OF SPANIARD series to allow classroom use, including homeschooling. Below are educational standards that this book can help meet with information in the story and related discussions. There are also questions to ask students before and after reading the book so you can measure understanding gained.

- Spaniard

Educational Area: TECH DEVICES

Helping students understand basics of technological devices, computer communications such as texting and email and related safe communication practices

QUESTION 1

What are some good things to do if you receive a text from an unknown number?

Educational Area: WORK AND EARNINGS

Helping students understand the business basic of profit and loss.

QUESTION 2

Could a lemonade stand become a lifelong business? Compare how money comes into the business (purchases and any other income) and how it goes out (business expenses). Why does more money have to come in than goes out? NOTE: After reading the story, you could discuss income and expenses for a company making action figures, such as the character Max runs.

FOR USING THIS BOOK WITH STUDENTS

Educational Area: PHYSICAL ACTIVITY

Helping students identify reasons to maintain physical fitness and physical activities that help.

QUESTION 3

Why do professional athletes and other serious sports competitors often have well-defined muscles? Why do other people sometimes want well-defined muscles?

Educational Area: HISTORY/SOCIAL STUDIES

Helping students understand how customs and culture differ across groups, and behaviors that sometime result, ranging from fear and dislike of the unfamiliar to the adoption of new practices.

QUESTION 4

The Spaniard has many tattoos. Is a tattoo a custom? Why do some people dislike tattoos? Have you been to Spain? What are examples of its culture? Has Spain changed life in other countries? NOTE: A useful related article in Wikipedia is "List of Spanish Inventions and Discoveries"

Educational Area: BALANCING FAMILY, WORK & COMMUNITY RESPONSIBILITIES

Helping students understand how to resolve and prevent conflict by using interpersonal communication skills, such as active listening, checking for understanding, and practicing empathy.

QUESTION 5

What is a good thing to do if you think someone misunderstands something about you?

BALANCING RESPONSIBILITIES *(continued)*
Helping students understand how to find solutions by analyzing consequences of alternative solutions, as opposed to making snap decisions.

QUESTION 6
What are some good things to do when you have to make a decision?

BALANCING RESPONSIBILITIES *(continued)*
Helping students understand that solving dilemmas includes learning from decisions by reflecting on them and drawing conclusions.

QUESTION 7
What are some ways to understand whether you made a good or bad decision?

Educational Area: SCIENCE, TECHNOLOGY AND HUMAN ENDEAVORS

Helping students understand how human needs lead to inventions that sometimes widely influence society.

QUESTION 8

Guess the answers to these questions if you don't already know: What is 3D printing? Why was 3D printing invented? Is 3D printing changing how we live?

Educational Area: CAREER ACQUISITION AND RETENTION

Helping students understand their personal interests and how these can often lead to careers or lifelong pursuits.

QUESTION 9

What are some of your personal interests? Toys? Sports? Computers? Something else? How might your greatest interests be part of your work and life in the future?

GETTING & KEEPING A CAREER *(continued)*

Helping students understand how their approaches to daily activities help prepare them for their future work and personal lives. For instance, how they practice commitment, cooperation, dependability, initiative, leadership, literacy and time management.

QUESTION 10

Think about a time when you failed at something that mattered to you. What did you do then? What will you do after a failure in the future?

Made in the USA
Middletown, DE
27 October 2023

41360716R00044